# PRO-BLOGGING
# SECRETS

## STRATEGIES, TIPS, AND ANSWERS YOU NEED TO GROW YOUR BLOG AND EARN MORE MONEY

BOB LOTICH

ISBN: 0989894533
ISBN-13: 978-0-9898945-3-1

# TABLE OF CONTENTS

iv

# ACKNOWLEDGMENTS

Special thanks to these fine folks for providing some great suggestions for content included in this book:

Jeff Rose (goodfinancialcents.com)
Theresa Skrobanek (myagingandwellness.com)
KC Beavers (genxfinance.com)
Lindsey Knerl (knerlfamilymedia.com)
Glen Craig (freefrombroke.com)
Kelly Whalen (thecentsiblelife.com)
Jonathan Milligan (bloggingyourpassion.com)
Todd Tresider (financialmentor.com)
Greg Go (wisebread.com)
Doug Nordman (the-military-guide.com)
Paula Pant (affordanything.com)
Allison Jones (bigfaithbuilders.com)

# FOREWORD

My name is Bob, and I blog for a living. Every time I say or write that, I still feel a little surprised I get paid to do what I absolutely love. Prior to full-time blogging, I spent many years in various jobs that seemed to suck the life out of me. I felt completely trapped in my career path and memories of the florescent lights and cloth walls of my windowless cubicle still haunt me. ;)

I know some people probably enjoy life in corporate America, but it was not for me. And the years I spent there just help me to forever appreciate the freedom that comes with having the best job in the world!

I have made a nice, full-time living from my blog for the past five years and launched my first blog (ChristianPF.com) more than seven years ago. At the time of this writing, we have been incredibly blessed with more than 22,000,000 visitors to the blog since we began. I don't tell you this number to brag because, honestly I have no idea how we did it! ;)

What I do know is that most bloggers who find out about the blog's success start asking a lot of questions. So, I took the most common questions (along with some of my best secrets) and wrote this book.

So while every chapter isn't technically a question

and answer, it is based on a question I'm regularly asked. I tend to write very casually, almost as if we are having a conversation. And while each chapter is a different length, they're all very short and to the point. No fluff here!

If you haven't already, you may want to pick up the first book in this series, *How to Make Money Blogging: How I Replaced My Day Job With My Blog.* You can order it on Amazon.com, or you can get a free PDF version at BlogBusiness101.com.

That book is for newer bloggers (this one is not) and covers basics about SEO, getting traffic, making money, and a lot more, and is content that intentionally isn't covered in this book.

## The nonexistent roadmap to blogging success

A lot has changed since I began blogging, and millions more blogs have appeared since then. Even with all the changes, I see more potential and opportunity for bloggers today than ever before.

There are a lot of ways to skin a cat as they say (are there really?), and there are also many ways to increase an audience, get traffic, and make money with a blog. Some will take the exact opposite approach I use, and they will do very well with their blogs. The truth is there isn't any one "right" way to do most of this stuff. So, don't be afraid to try your crazy ideas and even do the opposite of what some of the "experts" suggest. I know I broke many "rules" and sometimes with great results.

Resist the frustration resulting from the lack of a far-reaching road map to blogging success. View it as an exciting entrepreneurial journey in which learning by trial and error pays great dividends.

Even so, I love step-by-step detailed instructions as much as the next guy, and I include as many step-by-step instructions in this book (with many screenshots) as possible. The difference is while I (or others) can provide step-by-step instructions for certain tasks, a total step-by-step on the two- to five-year journey to a successful blog contains way too many variables. It's like asking any other small business owner for a step-by-step plan to success in his business. He couldn't provide it, but he surely could give you some tips, tricks of the trade, and other advice to help you succeed, and that's what I intend to  provides with this book.

At the time of this writing, all the info and links are relevant. If you find that any of the sites have changed or no longer exist, please let me know so I can update them.

You can find all the resources, tools, and links mentioned in this book at our website: BlogBusiness101.com/links.

I wish you all the best on your blogging journey and hope this book provides some helpful tips to guide you along the way.

# HOW DO I GET STARTED BLOGGING?

Sorry, you bought the wrong book. Save this book for a little way down the road; it will become a lot more helpful to you then. In the meantime, my first book in this series will cover everything you need to know to get started, and it costs less than a dollar.

You can even pick up a free PDF version at BlogBusiness101.com.

If you don't want to get the book, I have a step-by-step tutorial that shows you how to create a blog in under an hour. You can see that tutorial here:

http://youtu.be/u4gunO49mlk

# GETTING MORE TRAFFIC

# HOW WE ADDED 20,000 LEGIT FACEBOOK FANS IN SEVEN MONTHS

Seven months ago (from the time of this writing), we had 13,000 Facebook fans. These 13,000 clicked "Like" during the previous five to six years of running the blog. Today, as I write this, there are 33,427 Facebook fans. And these are legit and engaged fans I should add, not something where you pay $5 to some spammy company to get 1,000 fans.

So, we added 13,000 fans over five+ years and then picked up 20,000 in about seven months. How did we do it?

We made a few key changes:

## 1. We stopped exclusively promoting our stuff

During the five-year phase, we pretty much posted only recent blog posts to the Facebook page. If you think about it, that's pretty selfish.

We weren't asking what the audience wanted to see on the page, we were just force feeding them the stuff we wanted them to see. As a result, it wasn't a very engaged community, and it didn't grow very quickly.

To change this, we began posting anything we thought our readers would find helpful, entertaining, or valuable in any way, regardless of whether or not it was perfectly "on topic" with our blog.

For example, we found that a lot of our Facebook audience responded well to inspiring quotes, encouraging Bible verses, funny pictures, questions, and helpful articles from other blogs as well as ours.

The key change here was that we went from posting about 95 percent self-promotional posts (links to our blog posts) to about 20 percent. The remaining 80 percent was just to give the fans what they wanted to see.

As we began adding content that our fans enjoyed more, they, in turn, liked, commented, and shared our content a lot more, which helped us get new fans.

And now that we have a more engaged audience, when we do post a link to a blog post of ours, it gets a lot more response.

## 2. Frequency of posting

Up until five months ago, we were posting one time per day, which isn't a bad frequency, but when I researched a bunch of Facebook pages that had large followings, I found what they had in common was that they all seemed to post a lot more than once a day. We settled on five times a day and spaced them out about every three to four hours.

I can tell you right now I don't think we would have done this if it weren't for Bufferapp.com. If you aren't aware, Buffer is a tool that lets you schedule your Facebook, Twitter, G+, and even LinkedIn posts. It's free to start and highly recommended.

A note on quality over quantity. While we did step up our quantity, we worked hard to make sure the quality was great for everything we posted. I don't know all the ins and outs of Facebook's algorithm (it's always changing anyway), but at this point the posts that have the most engagement seem to be rewarded by being shown to more fans. So, it's to your benefit to try to always post stuff that your audience responds to.

# 3. Images for everything

Another thing we learned is that posts always performed better for us with an image. When posting a link to our blog post, rather than just pasting the link and letting Facebook pull in the blog post info, we found that posting the image from the blog post and then adding a link afterwards consistently performed a lot better. At the time of this writing, a pasted link shows up like this:

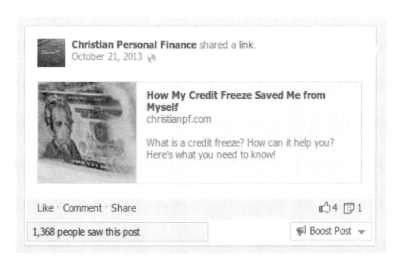

And a posted image (from the blog post) with a link added after shows like this:

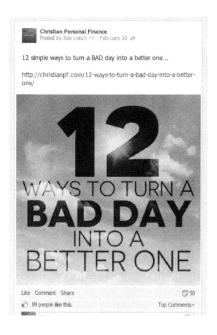

As you can see, it takes up a whole lot more real estate and, as a result, we've always had more engagement from the fans.

Also, when we post quotes, rather than just posting them as text, we find or create a graphic like this:

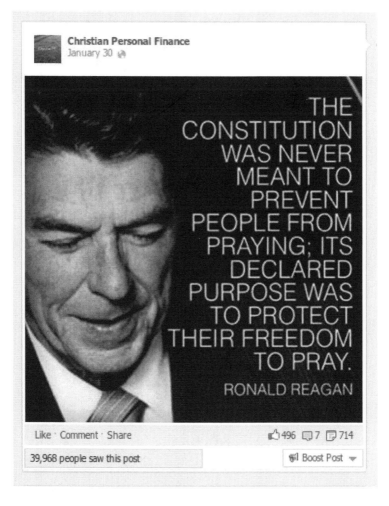

or like this:

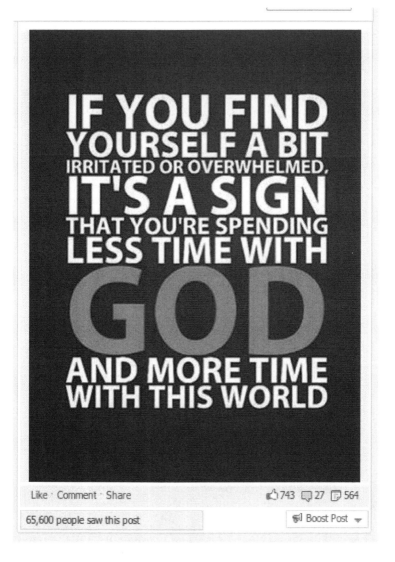

These also significantly outperformed just pasting in a text quote.

Now the obvious next question is, "How can I make image quotes like that?" And while I normally use Photoshop, there are some fantastic free tools that make this very easy.

Check out:

- Pinstamatic.com
- Idpinthat.com
- imgflip.com/memegenerator
- Canva.com

# 4. A few things to experiment with

Adding a request to "like" or "share" when posting something to Facebook works very well for some other pages, but you have to stay tasteful and not get aggressive with it. The jury is still out for us, but so far, it seems to help.

- Posting relevant videos
- Trivia questions
- Fill in the blank questions
- Yes or no questions

The bottom line is that the way we managed to grow our page by 20,000 fans in seven months is by working hard to get the audience to engage in some way. Comments and "likes" are great, but "shares" are what we're really after because that's when the viral magic happens. We tend to see the biggest number of fans added on the days one of our posts goes viral.

# TWO MORE SIMPLE WAYS TO GROW YOUR FACEBOOK AUDIENCE

In the previous chapter, I talked about what we did on our Facebook page to increase our audience, and that has, by far, had the biggest impact on our fan base. But, we did some simple things on our blog that played an important part of that growth, as well.

## 1. Put a Facebook "like" box in your sidebar

It's really as simple as it seems and will help you make progress growing your fan base. This was the only way we expanded our fan page for years. It's nowhere as effective as what we mentioned in the previous chapter, but still good nonetheless.

## 2. Put a "like" button on your thank you page

Start by finding the people who are buying, subscribing, commenting on, or sharing your material. These engaged folks are already excited about your blog, and they're apt to like your page on Facebook, too.

If you have a thank you page (or something similar) that you send new subscribers/customers, just add a line asking them to show their support by liking your blog on Facebook. Then insert a simple "like" button. It takes just a few minutes, and you'll immediately see an increase in "likes."

# THREE ARTICLE IDEAS GUARANTEED TO GET LINKS AND SHARES

If you haven't figured it out yet, getting links and shares of your content is absolutely critical to your blog's success. You can write the best stuff in the world, but if no one is sharing or linking to it, then you will have a very hard time increasing your blog's readership.

I have found one of the easiest ways to get more links and shares is to give them. So always look for ways to link to others and help other people, and they will return the favor.

I have had good results with a few specific ideas along these lines.

One of my favorite ideas is to create an article like "The best dog training tips from 20 professionals" and then ask 20 dog trainers for their best tips and tell them that if they provide a response, you will link to their blogs. Once you publish, email them all to let them know it's live and thank them for their help. Many will share it and link to you. I have had very good success from doing articles like these. And I still almost always participate in these type of articles when I'm asked, and I also usually share it after it's live. The key is to really create something great that people WANT to share!

Similar but different enough is creating a post that highlights some of the best or most influential people in your niche. Make sure to follow up and email each of them after you publish. You will surely get the post shared.

Do an interview with an influential person in your niche. Be sure to email them when the interview goes live. I have found that most people you interview want to share that someone interviewed them, so it often is a win-win situation for each of you.

# HOW DO I GET MORE TRAFFIC FROM PINTEREST?

Here's the simplest thing you can do today to increase your Pinterest traffic.

## Make sure every post (especially popular ones) has a good image.

Ideally, an image with the title of the post as a text overlay works best.

Here are a couple of examples from my blog:

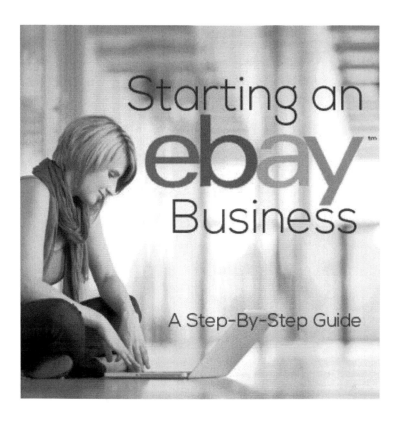

You can use images you find from stock photo sites or you could use a site like idpinthat.com, which allows you to find free images and add text right there.

Here's any example of how easy idpinthat.com is:

The Pinterest audience likes beautiful and informative images. Many of them use the site as a bookmarking tool, so the information (text) contained in the images is very important.

If you have hundreds of posts that don't have Pinterest-friendly images at this point, I would login to Google Analytics and on the left sidebar go to Behavior > Site Content > All Pages.

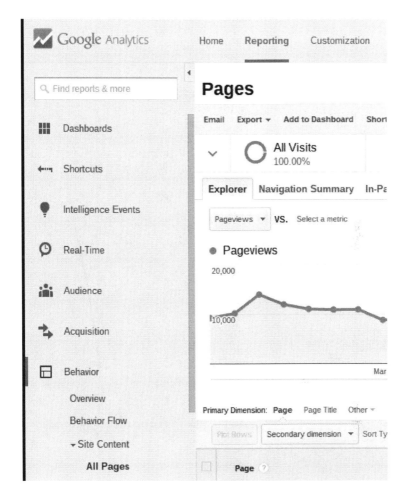

Now you will see your most trafficked posts. I'd start with these posts and make sure each has a pinnable image.

Now that you have Pinterest-friendly images on your site, let's make it even easier for your readers to pin them. You will want to install the "jQuery Pin It Button For Images" plugin. Once you do that, all the images on your site will automatically have a

"Pin It" button popup in the top left corner when someone hovers over it (as seen in the image below).

This is the simplest first step that any blogger should take if he or she wants to get more traffic from Pinterest.

There are countless other things you can do to drive more Pinterest traffic that are beyond the scope of this book, but here are a few more ideas to get you thinking.

- Create very specific (think long-tail) boards with target keywords included. Lots of people use Pinterest as a search engine now, and keywords matter.
- Create a board with your most popular posts and add it to your blog sidebar. The Pinterest

widget builder allows you to do this easily. ([business.pinterest.com/widget-builder](business.pinterest.com/widget-builder))

- Create infographics or tutorials within a single graphic.
- Join popular group boards and regularly pin your own posts but make sure you follow the rules of the board.

# IS COMMENTING ON BLOGS AND FORUMS WORTH THE TIME?

Blog and forum commenting still works. Sure, you won't likely get a thousand visitors from a single comment that you leave, but if you make a regular habit of commenting on related blogs and forums, you will see a small, but steady stream of traffic from those efforts.

More important than the direct traffic is the SEO-benefit of having links from a variety of different sites.

Regardless of whether or not someone follows the links, there are benefits, especially with Yahoo and Bing. The key is to comment on multiple sites related to your niche.

My good friend Jonathan Milligan showed me a tool that makes it a lot easier to find new sites to comment on. It is called DropMyLink.com, and all you need to do is provide a relevant keyword, and it will find related sites for you to comment on.

It should go without saying that when commenting you must add value. Don't just leave "great post!" comments. Read the post and leave a thoughtful and helpful comment for the most benefit.

# HOW DO I FIND BLOGS TO GUEST POST ON?

I talked a bit about guest posting in the previous book in this series, and I mentioned that it was one of my favorite ways to get traffic and increase an audience. While I think it's a little more difficult to do today than it was a few years ago, it's still well worth the effort and should remain high on your to-do list.

The absolute best way to guest post is to post with bloggers you have a relationship with. Your odds of getting your post published dramatically improve when you do it this way.

So, just like any other relationship advice you'd get, you shouldn't make your first impression just by asking for a favor. First, introduce yourself. Try to be helpful and make yourself useful. Be a friend. Then, offer to guest post and make it as beneficial for the other blogger as possible but don't be pushy.

Blog commenting is always a good way to start a relationship with other bloggers, but you should also find out where they spend time online. Are they always on Twitter? Retweet their stuff. Are they always on Facebook? Share something from page and tag them. Also, try to email them with any kind of helpful feedback you can provide. You get the picture. The goal is to connect with them on a personal level and put the time and energy into the relationship before asking for the favor.

So, now that we have the approach and method out of the way, let's chat a little about finding new bloggers who you can connect with.

To find some new bloggers, let's go to Google and try this search:

"related keyword" "guest post"

Replace "related keyword" with a similar keyword to your niche and try a few different variations. For example:

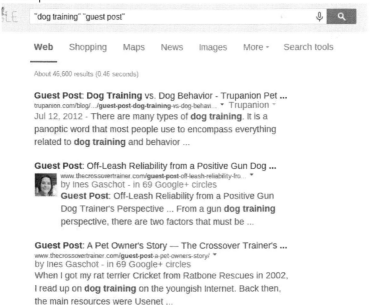

This search will almost always yield good results. What's great about it is that it will likely put you in touch with some bloggers you may not yet know as well as point you to bloggers who have accepted guest posts in the past.

If you have your sights set on a couple of big blogs and you aren't sure whether they accept guest posts, you can run this search at Google:

site:blogname.com "guest post"

Replace "blogname.com" with the blog you're trying to get info about. This search will reveal any instances of the phrase "guest post" on the blog. For example:

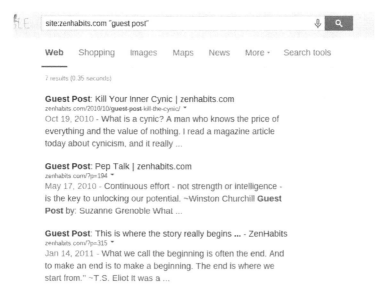

# CONTENT CREATION

# MY CHECKLIST AFTER I HIT PUBLISH

I have a relatively simple checklist I like to follow:

- Check for formatting issues once it goes live.

- Add to Buffer (bufferapp.com) and share to Linkedin, Google+, and Tweet three times during the next month.

- Find any old, related articles on my site and link from them to the newly published article.

- Pin the post on an appropriate board on Pinterest using Viraltag.com (a Buffer type tool specifically for Pinterest)

- If it's helpful or relevant to any media contacts/bloggers/etc. I know, I send a no-pressure email letting them know about it.

- I email anyone I linked to within the article letting them know I mentioned them.

- Add to the Facebook page creating an image post using the image in the article and then including the title and the link like this:

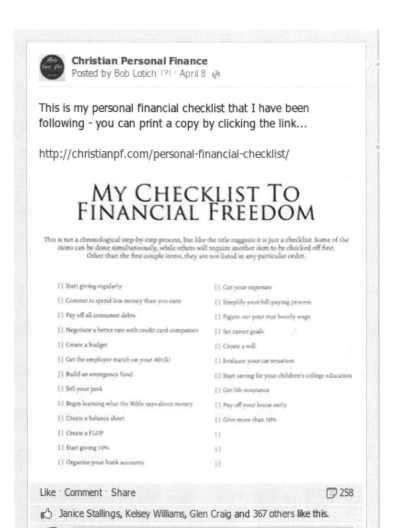

# WHY YOU HAVE TO STOP WRITING FOR OTHER BLOGGERS

One of the mistakes I've seen so many bloggers make over the years is that they write for their peers (other bloggers in their niche) instead of for their readers. With any craft or skill, there's often an elite group that's dismissive of beginners, and as such, many bloggers fall into the trap of writing to impress their peers.

While there's nothing wrong with writing in-depth and thorough pieces, you have to remember whom you're writing for. If technical and complicated is what your audience craves, then give it to them. But, if you have an audience that's mostly beginners (which most of us have), and you regularly write posts geared toward experts, you will quickly shrink the size of your audience.

It's OK if other bloggers don't think you're as cool or cutting edge because you're writing content geared toward the beginners.

Here's a little secret: For any skill that's learned, most

people are beginners. Therefore, this is the biggest audience that's up for grabs.

So stop trying to please/impress other bloggers and give your readers what they want!

# HOW DO YOU COME UP WITH BLOG POST IDEAS?

I have a variety of methods I use, but these are some of my favorites:

## 1. Ask Amazon

If you head over to Amazon.com, select "books" from the search bar and start by typing in a variety of basic and more specific topics that fall into your niche to get some ideas.

As you dig around, you may find a bunch of books with titles that may give you some great blog post ideas. Oftentimes, a book title could just as easily turn into a huge resource blog post you could write.

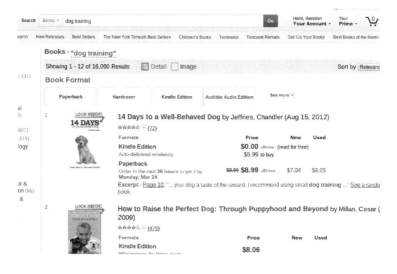

For example, if I follow this "dog training" thread, I find books titled:

- *14 Days to a Well-Behaved Dog*
- *How to Raise the Perfect Dog*
- *101 Dog Tricks*
- *How to Housebreak Your Dog in 7 Days*
- *Training Crazy Dogs*
- *How to Raise a Puppy*

With a little tweaking and research, I could create blog posts out of each of these. And the great news is that you already know these are in-demand topics because they rank so high on Amazon.

## 2. Check out related magazine covers

Magazine editors spend a lot of time and energy trying to figure what articles will draw in new readers. They post the best ones on the cover of each issue.

# 3. Read other blogs and websites

This is especially important if your niche has lots of changes like cell phones or politics. But even if you're writing about a more evergreen topic like gardening, it's still good to visit other websites, blogs, videos, etc. to get ideas.

# 4. Write about what bothers you

I don't do this often enough, but showing emotion and your human side is always a good way to connect with readers. And one of the best ways is to write about what frustrates you. Be it how GMOs are destroying our food, how Rand Paul is so much better than the other politicians, how wrong it is to cut down trees, or any other topic that people get passionate about. Writing about topics you care about will certainly offend some and you'll lose some readers, but at the same time, it will add a much stronger bond with you and your followers.

# 5. Reader questions

If you have a contact form or your email address listed on your contact page (which I recommend having and Contact Form 7 is a great plugin for that), then you'll get questions from readers. And when you get a question, you can bet that many other readers have that same exact question. Not only will these make great and relevant blog posts, but they also show your readers you're listening.

# HOW DO YOU FIND GOOD KEYWORDS FOR YOUR BLOG POSTS?

One of the essential elements of SEO for bloggers is to have a keyword phrase that you're targeting with your blog posts. It's OK not to target a phrase with every post, but if you want to get traffic from the search engines, it's wise to focus on keywords for at least half of your blog posts.

Strategically working this keyword into your title without sounding like a goofball is an art that requires a lot of practice, but the more you do it, the better you get at it. And with many blogs getting more traffic from social media than from Google, it's a good idea to focus on creating a title that's catchy and will do well on social media while including a keyword.

As far as finding keywords, I really like wordstream.com/keywords. It allows you to get 30 free searches to see if you like it.

I also still like and use wordtracker.com as my go-to site for keyword ideas.

Once you have your tool, you'll want to search very generic and broad terms about your topic. Pay close attention to the long-tail (more than three to four words) phrases, because these are almost always going to be easier to rank for.

I often like to combine two to three long-tail phrases to create my title because it gives me an opportunity to rank for all three of them.

For example:

When I was creating an article that was going to be listing a bunch of budgeting spreadsheets, I began my keyword research by searching for "budgeting spreadsheet." It was clear there were a ton of people searching for that phrase, but what was exciting was that there were a ton of long-tail related keywords, as well.

I noticed these long-tail phrases:

- Free budgeting spreadsheet
- Household budgeting spreadsheets

I then combined them and added a number to make it a list to create my keyword-targeted title "10 Free Household Budgeting Spreadsheets"

After getting some links to this post, I not only began ranking for these longer phrases, but over time, I began to rank for the original phrase "budgeting spreadsheet," as well.

# MAKING
# MONEY

# MY BLOG EARNINGS HAVE PLATEAUED. WHAT SHOULD I DO?

I believe 99 percent of blogs out there (which are trying to earn more) are grossly under-monetized. I personally feel this is a skill that, if learned, would send many blogs from part-time income to full-time in a matter of months.

But like any other skill, it requires a lot of hard work and practice.

As a professional blogger (that still makes me laugh saying that out loud), people seem to think I don't really work, I just write an article occasionally and then sit on Facebook or watch talk shows all day.

The truth is, if you want to really make money from your blog, you have to work hard, and as for me, I spent years figuring out how to make more from the traffic I was getting. And if there's anything I learned, it's that you can *always* make more money from the traffic you're currently getting.

The key becomes figuring out how far you're willing

to go. For me, the super-aggressive ads like pop-unders, popups, etc. were just not worth the money. They pay very well, but they kill the site's professionalism and user experience, and that just wasn't a trade I was willing to make.

But, don't forget there are always ways to make more money from your blog. The more time and energy you spend uncovering and discovering the hidden potential, the more you will earn.

The next couple of chapters go over some quick hits and fairly easy tricks and techniques you can implement today.

# HOW CAN I EARN MORE WITH ADSENSE? – PART 1

For years, I've told bloggers that if they simply start testing different variations with their Adsense units, they can increase their earnings over night.

Those who took me up on it have confirmed there's a lot of money left on the table. But for those who don't ever do testing, I assume it's because it seems too difficult to figure out how to do it.

Well, Adsense has finally made it very easy for us to test a lot of different variations right from the Adsense dashboard.

First, log in to your Adsense account and click the "My Ads" tab. On the left side, click "Experiments."

This will lead you to a page that looks like this:

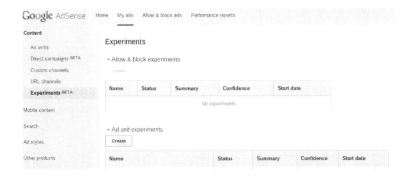

Now, hit the "Create" button to get started on your first variation.

Now, you can fill out the title and details of what you want to test. I suggest testing different colors of links, display ads vs. text ads, and, possibly, fonts.

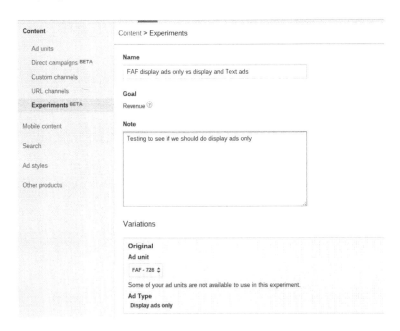

Under the "Variations" area, select an ad unit you

would like to test. To get the quickest results I suggest testing your most popular ad unit first.

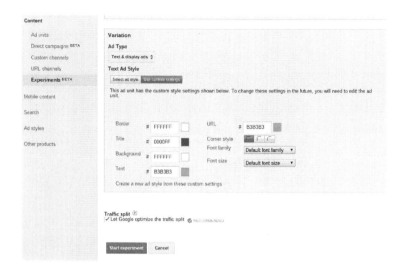

In this particular test, I'm testing display ads compared to text and display ads. The original is display ads only, and for this variation, I just need to fill out how I want my text ads to appear.

After that's complete, you just need to hit "Start Experiment," and Google does the rest of the work for you. Google will auto-confirm the winner after you give enough impressions. Or you can end the test at any point if you feel there's a good enough chance that one is better than the other.

Here are my results from a test I started 28 days ago where I tested the link color:

If you look at the test above in the comparison column, you can see how much better one ad is performing than the other. In the revenue column, you get to actually see what that equates to in dollars per 1,000 impressions. (By the way, I have that info whited out in the image above because it's against Adsense TOS to share that info.)

But the bottom line here is that changing the color of my links in my ad increased my revenue by 80 percent!

The test isn't officially over yet, but since this unit has gotten almost 200K impressions, I'm comfortable we have a clear winner. So, now all I need to do is click the "Choose" next to the winner, and Adsense will automatically start showing that ad exclusively.

# HOW CAN I EARN MORE WITH ADSENSE? – PART 2

The simple answer is that you want to place your ads in the best-paying locations.

A couple of years ago, the best advice to increase earnings was to cram as many ads above the fold as possible, but now in light of Google's Panda, we have to be a little more strategic with ad placement.

On the next page is the official layout guide from Adsense on where the best-paying locations are.

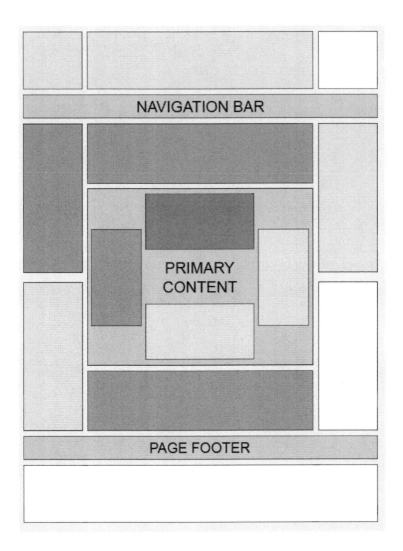

NAVIGATION BAR

PRIMARY
CONTENT

PAGE FOOTER

As you can see, the best-paying location is within the content.

I have tested this on probably a dozen blogs, and I consistently find it's true with my blogs. While there's no guarantee it will be the case for you, the chances are pretty good these will be the best-paying locations for your blog as well.

My best performing ad unit for years is directly below the title of my blog posts as seen below:

The second best place I have had a lot of success with placing ad units is in the middle of the article as shown below:

So the next question that always follows is, "How do I do that because there's no easy way to do that with

WordPress by default?"

Well, some time ago after dozens of hours of searching on how to do this, I found a plugin called Quick Adsense, and this is exactly what it does.

At the time of this writing, it still works very well with the current version of WordPress, and it's very easy to use as well.

As with everything, test, test, and then re-test. If these are new positions for you, please try them out and let me know how they do for you.

# HOW DO YOU GET THOSE UNIQUE SIZE ADSENSE UNITS THAT YOU HAVE ON YOUR BLOG?

Just recently, the Adsense team quietly rolled out custom-fit Adsense units. which means, as you can guess, that you can create a custom height and width of your ad unit.

All you need to do is to create a new ad unit, and when you do, you will notice the site now has the custom option, just select that and you're off to the races.

## The pros of using custom-sized ads

The first pro is they will likely look better. Unless you designed your blog around the common ad sizes, there are probably places where you have ad units that just don't quite fit as well as they could or you'd like. As a result, maybe they don't look as nice as one that fits well.

Second, they will help fight ad blindness. Adsense units haven't really changed their look in the past decade and so, almost everyone, including your grandma, can quickly identify them as ads and, consequently, will pay little attention to them. You now have the ability to break out of those old standard units and create a new size and shape that integrates nicely with your blog and may get more interaction from the readers.

## The cons of using custom-sized ads

Your ads will almost exclusively be text ads. Since banner advertisers only create so many different sizes (300x250, 728x90, and 160x600 are the most common), you can bet you'll see very few image ads in the 436x278 ad unit you created.

Because of the previous point, your earnings may suffer. Like everything, this is definitely worth testing to see if it legitimately hurts your earnings or not, but the Adsense folks do issue a warning that your earnings may drop when using these units.

I've used custom Adsense units as long as I've had access to them, and after testing on my site, I found no measurable earnings drop, and they fit better and looked better, so I've stuck with them.

# HOW I MADE AN EXTRA $1,000 A MONTH WITH FIVE MINUTES OF WORK

OK, this is a bit of a sensational chapter title, and just like *The 4-Hour Work Week* isn't a literal guide to a four-hour work week but rather a guide to move you in that direction, this chapter's goal is to show you a technique that will move you in that direction.

Even so, this technique did literally yield a bump of $1,000/month for me with just a few minutes of work. So, I hope you can use it to your advantage, as well.

I used Adsense to accomplish this, but in theory, any CPC ad network can yield the same results.

Start by going to your top 10 most trafficked articles and see who's showing up as advertisers. You may want to refresh the page a few times to see if different advertisers show up.

# ESTATE TAXES

As you can tell from this image, taxrates.com seems to be paying for advertising with Google on my site. What we now want to do is go over to their site.

Of course, don't click the ad since that's click fraud. Just type it into your browser window.

Now look around and see if the site has an affiliate program. Oftentimes, sites have links to the affiliate program at the bottom of the page. If you don't find one, send an email to ask whether they have one.

My biggest success with this method was from one of my highly trafficked pages. It was a small company that was extremely relevant to the post, and it did have an affiliate program. So I signed up, added an affiliate link to the post, and immediately started earning about $1,000/month just from those few minutes of work.

# HOW TO MAKE MORE MONEY WITH CJ.COM

These are three strategies that have served me well and helped me dramatically increase the earnings of my blogs.

## 1. Always look to see whether a site has an affiliate program

Just as we mentioned in the previous chapter, you should start getting in the habit of always checking to see whether the company you're linking to has an affiliate program. You'll probably be surprised at how many companies do have an affiliate or referral program of sorts. Start by checking the home page for a link to an affiliate's page, and if you don't find one, definitely follow up with an email.

I've learned that some companies have them but don't advertise them and keep them private. Then some poor companies don't even know what they are, and that gives you the opportunity to explain it to them and possibly be the first affiliate.

Just recently, I did this with a small company. I loved

the service that it offered and was already promoting it on my site, but I asked about the affiliate program and after a nice email exchange, the company ended up creating one just because I asked. It took maybe 30 minutes of work on my part and allowed me to turn those links I already had on my site into money-earning affiliate links.

## 2. Search CJ.com for ideas

One of my favorite ways to find new affiliate programs (and companies, for that matter) that I wasn't aware of is to search through CJ's list of advertisers.

Once you log in, click "Get Links" from the home page.

Next, you'll see a categorized list of advertisers:

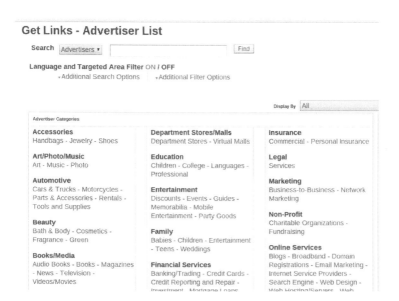

You should first find the most relevant categories and click to see what unknown advertisers or affiliate programs are available to you.

I regularly scour these listings and click and investigate any new companies that show up.

Just click the name of the company to get a more

detailed description of what it does and offers as well as a link to the home page.

Just from the list above, I'm already getting some ideas for my wedding blog (if I had one). I see photo-stamps, which would be an awesome idea for a post. What better way to customize your wedding invitation than to use a postage stamp with a photo of the happy couple?

Also, "My M&Ms" I understand allows you to create your own custom color combination of M&Ms. This would be perfect on the tables at a wedding reception or in goodie bags.

Each of these options is an interesting article on its own, but even if you didn't want to write articles specifically about these products, you could write something like "10 Ways to Customize Your Wedding" and find eight other clever ideas. (You could find these in five minutes on Pinterest.)

A list like this that just happens to mention a few interesting products could work very well since it's something readers want to share and since you have some affiliate links included, you have a chance to make some sales, as well.

## 3. Pull top posts in analytics and search CJ for affiliate links you can insert

This is my favorite way getting more out of my blog. Go to Google Analytics and then on the left sidebar click Behavior > Site Content > All Pages

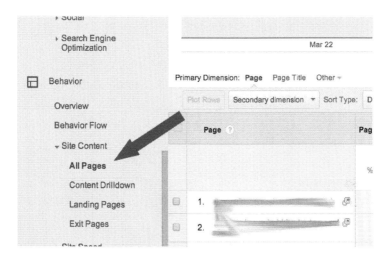

You will see a list of your posts and pages on your site with the most traffic. This is a great place to begin looking for affiliate-linking opportunities.

After all, these pages are getting traffic, so doesn't it make sense you should first focus your energy there?

Unless you stay on topic more than most bloggers I know, some of these posts will veer slightly off topic, and they may not fall into the category you searched for in CJ in the previous step. If not, then search for the appropriate category or use the search bar and see what comes up.

Next, ask yourself, why people are visiting the page. If you can understand their intent, then it will give you some great ideas on products that may be helpful for them.

Years ago, I created a post on one of my blogs called something like "Bible verses about death." After doing this exercise, and from reading the comments, it dawned on me that many of the visitors were coming to the page looking for verses to use in a eulogy they were working on. I did some digging and discovered an ebook that helped people write a great eulogy. And it had an affiliate program. I then put a link in the post just mentioning it as a potentially helpful resource. And it was, and people bought it, and I started making a little money from a post that hadn't really earned anything before.

A warning about affiliate marketing:

Stay pleasant and genuinely try to help your readers with the products you promote. And if you don't or wouldn't use it yourself, don't promote it.

I have found that the most success in affiliate marketing comes from looking for win-win situations. When you find a product that will really help your readers, you're on to something. If you're just pushing something on them because it pays a large commission, you will quickly chase all your loyal readers away.

Your job is to help make your readers' lives better, and the more you can do that, the more success you will have. This really applies to all aspects of blogging.

*"You can get everything in life you want if you will just help others get what they want." -Zig Ziglar*

# SHOULD I SELL PRODUCTS OR SERVICES FROM MY BLOG?

In a word: absolutely!

Honestly, the way I've monetized my blog (almost exclusively from ads) is one of the slowest ways to earn from your blog. I have seen other bloggers with FAR less traffic earn a full-time living by offering consulting and/or products on their blogs.

With rare exception, whatever you're blogging about, some readers out there are willing to pay you for your time, the products you created, or just to have your information in an easier to digest format like a book or a course.

It took me years to realize that my readers want the products I offer. I always thought they would just want it all for free, but really many of them would love to support your efforts. Also, they trust you and look to you as someone who can help them solve their problems. So, when you offer a product or service that will help them do that, you will make sales.

Although it may seem scary putting yourself out there, it's likely one of the best ways you can make a deep and lasting impact on your readers' lives, so decide to get over your fears and go for it.

# THE BUSINESS OF BLOGGING

# HOW DO I FORMALIZE MY BLOG AS A BUSINESS?

I get asked this question all the time, and while I'm not the most qualified to answer (talk with an accountant or a lawyer for the expert answer), I will share my experience in hopes it may help.

I started my first blog as a hobby in 2007, and I only made about $100 total with it the first six months, so a sole proprietorship was the perfect business entity.

*By the way, if you do nothing, you're automatically a sole proprietor. I didn't realize this when I started, but if you just start a business and don't form an LLC, S-corp, etc., then by default the IRS considers you a sole proprietor.*

Running the business as a sole proprietor is the cheapest and simplest because you don't have to do anything different. You just mark your business earnings on your tax return along with your income from your day job, etc.

I ran my business as a sole proprietor for about a year

and a half until I formed a single-member LLC. There are a few different options when choosing your business entity, but I chose the LLC for a couple of reasons.

## 1. It was simple to run.

As a single-member LLC, I didn't need to divide the percentage of ownership. Really, not much changed from running the sole proprietorship as far as what I needed to do to maintain it. I still get to use a single tax form, instead of one for the business and one for personal.

## 2. An LLC offers legal protection.

After doing a bit of research, it became pretty clear that an LLC is safer than a sole proprietorship. From what I understand, the biggest downside of being a sole proprietor is that you don't have much legal protection. So if your business gets sued, the plaintiff (the person suing you) can take your house. That's no fun.

## 3. It proves to the IRS that you mean business.

Apparently, there are a lot of people who create home-based "businesses" just so they can write off expenses like a computer, desk, etc. The IRS is good at what it does (i.e. spotting illegitimate businesses), and I remember reading an article that claimed the likelihood of an audit decreases by 90 percent for

LLCs rather than sole proprietors.

So again, I recommend chatting with an accountant and a lawyer to find out what would be best for your situation both from a tax benefit standpoint as well as from a legal protection.

# HOW TO GET AN LLC THE CHEAP WAY

I knew a lawyer who helped me through the process, but if you aren't so lucky and don't have a $1,000 ready to spend on lawyer fees, you can use an online legal service like RocketLawyer.com.

There are many sites like it, but this site helps you to form an LLC at a much lower price than with a lawyer face to face.

As you can see in the following image the total cost (for my state) comes out to $433.95, but if we take a closer look, you will see that you can get it quite a bit cheaper by not using some of the optional services.

| Pricing table | |
| --- | --- |
| **Item** | **Price** |
| Processing Fee | $99.95* |
| State Filing | $125.00 |
| Registered Agent (optional) | $99.00 |
| Tax ID (optional) | $40.00 |
| Corporate Kit (optional) | $70.00 |
| *Free with Pro Legal Plan enrollment. | |

# The registered agent

All corporations and LLCs must have a registered agent, a person or business able to receive documents during normal business hours at a legal physical location within the business' state. Since I'm at my business location during regular business hours, I chose to be my own registered agent and saved the fee. Some people may need this, but, surely, some will not.

# The tax ID (or EIN)

This one is a joke. You can apply for an EIN online for free. (See the next chapter.) It literally is a five-minute process, and then you have your Tax ID. No one needs to pay $40 for this.

# The corporate kit

This is just a bunch of junk (in my opinion) to get you to spend more. Some people may want it, but you can find and purchase it all separately.

According to the website, *"The corporate kit memorializes your new business. It has all the essential tools to get your company started: embossed binder, stock certificates, sample bylaws, business forms, and more."*

# Final thoughts

If you can do without those things and happen to live in Missouri like me (each state's filing fee is different), you can get it all done for $225 at RocketLawyer.com.

# HOW TO GET A TAX ID OR EIN FOR FREE

As you get going in your blogging endeavors, you'll probably want to get an EIN (Employer Identification Number). Even for bloggers who aren't making much money, it still might be good just so you don't have to use your Social Security Number every time you sign up with an ad network.

According to the IRS website:

*"This EIN is your permanent number and can be used immediately for most of your business needs, including opening a bank account, applying for business licenses, and filing a tax return by mail."*

## Get an EIN for free!

What I'm finding is that many people don't know you can get an EIN for free. Actually, I didn't know that either when I got mine; I think I paid $45 to some company to get it. And just today, I was talking to someone who was going to pay $80 to get one.

The good news for us all is that you can just go to the IRS website and use its online application and within about five minutes, you'll have a PDF approval letter showing your newly created EIN for your business – without spending a dime.

## Get your EIN now

Want to get one now? You won't believe how easy it is. Just follow these simple steps when applying for an EIN number:

- Go to the IRS EIN page (http://www.irs.gov/Businesses/Small-Businesses-&-Self-Employed/Apply-for-an-Employer-Identification-Number-(EIN)-Online) and scroll down to the bottom and click the link that says "APPLY ONLINE NOW."
- You will find the EIN number application.
- Click the "Begin Application" button to apply for EIN number
- Answer about 10 to 15 quick questions

That's it. You just got a free EIN number.

Note: Be warned that if you leave your computer for 15 minutes during the application process, the EIN website will kick you out, and you have to start over.

After you submit your application, you get a PDF document with your EIN. I suggest saving that somewhere safe, just so you don't forget it.

It isn't very easy to look up your EIN number once you forget it (most websites out there want to charge you to do an EIN lookup), so save yourself the hassle and don't forget it.

## Apply for an EIN over the phone

If you have trouble with the online EIN application process or just feel more comfortable on the phone, you can call the IRS and apply for an EIN over the phone at (800) 829-4933 from 7:00 a.m. to 10:00 p.m. (Eastern time).

# HOW DO I KEEP PEOPLE FROM STEALING MY CONTENT?

The short answer is you can't.

If you haven't noticed yet, it's very difficult to police the Internet. It is, after all, the World Wide Web, and it's hard enough tracking down all the bad guys in the U.S., let alone the rest of the world.

When I first started blogging and I found that other sites had reprinted my articles without my permission, it drove me crazy. To make matters worse, the sites often didn't have any contact information, so I couldn't even email them to ask them to remove it.

After this happened dozens of times, I began to realize these sites were just spam sites, and no one ever visited them anyway. So even though I hadn't given them permission and didn't really want them stealing my content, it really wasn't hurting me much.

There were a few occasions, where other bloggers innocently enough (giving them the benefit of the doubt) plagiarized/reprinted some of my articles without my permission. In every one of these instances, a simple email requesting that they remove it took care of the issue.

After being at this for seven years now, I don't worry about it anymore, as a general rule. A lot of sites have stolen my content over the years, and I don't really think it has hurt me in the least. I have come to terms with it, and while I do try to minimize plagiarism when possible, I don't lose any sleep over it anymore.

If you find yourself in a situation and you think your stolen content is harming your blog, go to DMCA.com and file a takedown request. This should get it taken care of, but personally, I reserve this for extreme cases; otherwise, you may find yourself spending way too much time filling out these forms.

# WILL I GET SUED IF I JUST USE GOOGLE IMAGES TO FIND IMAGES FOR BLOG POSTS?

It is quite possible, friend.

Do yourself a favor and do NOT use images from Google for your blog posts. I see way too many bloggers doing this and while you may get away with it for a while, it will most likely catch up to you in the future.

The issue is that Google images (even when using the filters) contain copyrighted photos and using them will get you in trouble.

Case in point: A few months ago, I got a letter from the wonderful legal team at Getty images requiring me to pay $750 for an image I had used without a license on an old blog post of mine that no one even read.

For the past five years or so, I've been good about only using images that were Creative Commons-licensed or that I had purchased the rights to use. So I was a bit confused as to how this happened. After pulling up the offending blog post, I realized that the image referred to was actually part of a screenshot I took from Turbotax on a review post.

So, technically, Turbotax did (I assume) have the legal right to use the image, and I took a screenshot of the Turbotax site. Also, the total size of the screenshot was about 200px by 200px, which put the actual image size the Getty lawyers were concerned about to probably 25px by 25px.

So after seeing all this, I hoped they would have some leniency given the circumstances, and they did. I called the number on the threatening letter, and the person I talked to said he'd let it slide if I removed the image from my site.

I learned some big lessons here, but the biggest was that these guys are using bots to scour the Web looking for unlicensed images. Since that's the case, no one and no website, no matter how old or unpopular, is safe.

I thought they only accidentally stumble on a popular post and say, "Hey, I think that's my image he's using," but instead, they have the tools to scour every nook and cranny of the Internet looking for violators.

So, how do you find free legal images? Hang on just a bit, we will cover that in later chapters.

# HOW DO I PROTECT MY SITE FROM HACKERS AND OTHER THREATS?

1. Always keep WordPress and plugins updated to the newest version. So when WordPress is reminding you to update to the new version, do it ASAP rather than waiting. The older versions expose website vulnerabilities. Think of it like a broken lock on your front door, which makes it a lot easier for the bad guys.

2. Regularly back up your blog and the database. You can never eliminate all risk of something happening to your blog, so the wise move is to regularly back it up.

3. Change your admin name. If you login with the username "admin" (or if the admin user even exists), you should delete that username and create a new one, ideally not your first name, either. If hackers know your user name, they have half the puzzle already solved.

4. Install the "Limit Login Attempts" plugin. This plugin will lock out a user after X number of failed login attempts. The plugin allows you to adjust the number, just in case you're forgetful. Without this plugin, spambots can keep trying 30,000 password combinations until they get it right.

## A tool I like

If you're looking for a way to automate some of this, I recommend the folks at Vaultpress.com. They run a service that automatically backs up your site files and database for you each day. The site also has a security-monitoring feature that monitors your blog for security threats, malicious code, and hack attempts. The service starts at $5/month.

# DO I REALLY HAVE TO INCLUDE MY HOME ADDRESS IN ALL MY EMAILS TO MY SUBSCRIBERS?

According to the CAN-Spam Act of 2003, you do have to include a mailing address in your emails. If you don't feel comfortable using your home address (I can't say I blame you), you can rent a P.O. box from your local post office for as cheap as $10/month, depending on your ZIP code.

An even better option is to rent a box from the UPS store, which allows you to have items and mail shipped there that can't be shipped to a P.O. box. My local UPS store charges only slightly more than my post office and offers more features like allowing after-hours pickup and email notifications when I receive mail.

# THE TOP 10 PLUGINS I CAN'T LIVE WITHOUT

## Quick Adsense

I mentioned this one earlier in the Adsense chapters, and at the time of this writing, it's my favorite, and for the longest time, the only way to get ad units in the middle of the blog post. And if you've forgotten from the earlier chapters, those ads typically perform very well embedded in the content. This plugin makes is possible and very easy.

## Yoast SEO

If you're using the Studiopress Genesis theme that I use, love, and recommend, you may not need this, but it's helpful. It's an all-in-one plugin that gives you a ton of SEO knobs to twist and turn that will help your site.

## Advanced Lazy Loading

If you have a lot of images in your posts, this site is a big help. This plugin will help reduce the page load time while opening the images as the user scrolls rather than all at once.

## Flare

This plugin allows you to embed all the social buttons (Facebook, Twitter, G+, etc.) on your posts, and it looks gorgeous, as well. I have a hard-coded hybrid approach I'm using right now. Otherwise I'd definitely use this one.

## Nrelate Related Content

This is a related content plugin that gives you many options on how to show related posts from your site on individual blog posts. There are a bunch of these out there, but this is the one that worked well for me.

## OptinMonster

This is a premium plugin ($50 for the basic version) that allows a beautiful popup on your site to new visitors to encourage them to join your email list. It's very easy to customize and has a lot of options as well.

## Scribe

This is a premium SEO plugin that probably isn't worth the cost for most bloggers; it starts at $97/month. But it's pretty awesome and allows you to do all your keyword research, analysis, and a lot more right from your WordPress dashboard.

# Search Regex

This is a utility plugin I have found is a lifesaver. It allows you to search and replace a word or phrase anywhere on your site. It has come in very handy for me from time to time.

# pTypeConverter

pType Converter is another utility plugin that allows you to change a post to a page or a page to a post. Most people will probably never need this, but if you do, it's nice to know it exists.

# WordPress Editorial Calendar

If you like to stay organized, this plugin makes it possible to see all your posts on a monthly calendar and drag and drop them to change the publish date.

# HOW DO I KEEP EMAIL FROM EATING UP ALL MY TIME?

This isn't a time management book, but I suggest finding ways to minimize the amount of time you check email. I'm not nearly as extreme as Tim Ferriss and his one-time per week email checking schedule, but if you want to be productive, you simply can not have email open all day.

The key is to batch the email process. I'm willing to bet that you don't regularly wash one sock at a time or bake one cookie at a time. Am I right? The reason you don't is that it's extremely inefficient. You end up spending a whole lot more time washing each sock as it becomes dirty than you would when you batch the process. Email is no different. And for some reason, many people use email in the most inefficient way possible.

If that weren't reason enough to change your email habit, consider all the lost productivity you suffer by being "in the zone" with a task you were working on when a new email popped up and interrupted you every few minutes. Many people spend every workday like this and then wonder why they never seem to get anything accomplished.

The good news is that even slight improvements in disciplining your email addiction can yield big productivity results. Even if you can't make drastic changes at this point, start by closing your email while working on important tasks to eliminate the distraction, if only for an hour or two.

Something that has worked well for me is to identify my single most important task I need to accomplish that day. When I get it completed, I "reward" myself by checking email.

This simple trick helps give me more incentive to get important tasks done, allows me to do them without the distraction of email, and also forces me to batch my email process.

# DELEGATION

# HOW DO I FIND PEOPLE TO HIRE?

This is so tough. It's like finding someone who's worthy of dating your daughter. Is anyone really good enough?

The fact of the matter is that you can't do everything yourself. While I think being a jack-of-all-trades is an essential characteristic of entrepreneurs, we still have to know when we need help. I have tried a few different ways of hiring help over the years, and these are my thoughts.

## Fiverr.com

This site is great because you can hire help for all kinds of tasks from logo creation, to voiceover work, to social media submissions all for $5. That's also why this site is not great. I have found that generally you get what you pay for with Fiverr.com. But for $5, it may be worth the risk. I definitely wouldn't hire any business-critical help here like a web-developer editing PHP on your blog, but if your budget is small, you can maybe find some decent affordable help.

# Odesk.com and Elance.com

I have hired a handful of workers from Odesk.com and Elance.com, and I have had some wins and some losses. The key is to find someone who's knowledgeable in exactly what you want him or her to do. Ideally, you want someone who has done (and has reviews to prove it) the exact thing you want to hire them for.

For example, I want a site redesign for my blog. I search for someone with lots of five-star reviews who's an expert in WordPress, CSS, PHP, and the specific theme (if you use a premium theme). I also look at the portfolio and ideally only choose a candidate if he or she has done a redesign I can point to and say, "I want it to look like that."

A quick note about working with designers: There's an inherent communication challenge between the visionary (yourself) and the designer. When all you can give them is, "I want it to feel fresh and exciting," you're asking for trouble. It makes the designer's life so much easier (and yours as well) when you can point to specific design elements you like.

My last redesign I took screenshots of design elements from various blogs and sites I liked and sent them to the designer. I sent him screenshots of different fonts I liked, footer layouts, sidebar layouts, graphic elements, etc. It allowed him to do his job much faster, and we avoided a lot of the back and forth of his guessing at what I really wanted.

# Ask your audience.

I used this method a few times, and it yielded great results. Even if you have a relatively small audience, you have a group of people who are interested and passionate about the same topic as you. This is a great place to find help. You could write a simple blog post letting your readers know you're looking for a person to help with _____, and they need to have these specific qualifications. With the job market what it is right now, you will likely find your readers will share it with their friends and family who they know might be a good fit.

# SHOULD YOU HIRE WRITERS FOR YOUR BLOG?

I made the decision early on that I wanted my site's brand to stand on its own two feet, apart from me. This is actually a tougher road than allowing yourself (the blogger) to be the brand because it's a lot easier for people to connect with a blogger than a brand. But, my focus wasn't just to make a living, but to build a site that could passively earn me money and that I could sell if it ever came to it. I knew having it focused around the idea of the site rather than the "Bob Lotich" show would make it much easier to accomplish my goals.

So when people ask me if/when they should hire writers, it's a tough question to answer because it truly comes down to a matter of strategy and what direction you want the site to follow.

The simple truth is that if all your readers come to your site because of you, then hiring writers may not be the best approach, or, at least, you can expect some growing pains.

When we brought on our first writer, I didn't get any negative comments from readers about it, and I was thrilled with the extra time it provided me. Shortly after that, I brought on about six more writers, and I knew there would probably be some kickback from the readers, but I knew it was what I needed to do to move myself more into a management position for the site and pursue bigger picture goals rather than focusing all my energy on writing blog posts each week.

There were a few comments from readers asking where I had gone, but all in all, it was an easy transition. And with all the extra time I had to work on growing the site, it was definitely worth it.

But all of the things I was scared of, like traffic dropping, subscribers leaving, tons of email complaints about it, never happened. In fact, I think it was actually better for the site, because I found writers who could cover topics I maybe wasn't as strong in and could provide value to the readers I couldn't.

But as I said before, the downside with this model is that there isn't as strong a "connection" between the readers and our blog as there maybe is if I were the sole voice of it.

I suggest spending some time and thinking about which direction you want to go before making the leap.

# HOW DO I FIND WRITERS WHO UNDERSTAND MY VISION AND CAN ACTUALLY WRITE WELL?

I tried a few different methods, and I definitely have a favorite. But I will go over all the things I tried to give you a little insight.

## 1. Hired writers from Textbroker.com

This is a pretty cool site. You can hire writers to write about a specific topic of your choice, and you pay only when you're happy with the article. There are all skill levels of writers available, and they're priced accordingly.

While there are some great applications for a tool like this, I found that none of the writers could write in the style I was looking for, perhaps a bit more personal. All the ones I tried just tended to write as if they were writing a textbook. It was way too formal for my taste. I tried coaching them and tried out quite a few, and it just didn't work out. So your luck may vary, but that was my experience.

## 2. Problogger job forums

For another blog of mine, I went to the ProBlogger job boards and took out a $50 ad and posted a detailed request of what I was looking for in writers and said I was offering $25 per article.

I was overwhelmed with the response. I got more than 200 people interested in the position. I would say at least half of them weren't qualified, but there were probably 10 to 20 I thought might fit well. I ended up taking the best six (though I only needed three writers) assuming that some of them may not last too long.

This ended up yielding good results and I would do it again, if needed. My suggestion if you do decide to take out an ad with forums like these is to be as descriptive as possible about what type of person you are, article topics, and anything else you want.

## 3. Hire from your reader base

By far the best place to find qualified writers who share your passion for the topic is from your readership. I had heard this repeated to me again and again and didn't really believe it until I tried it.

The way we found great writers from our reader base was to hold a writing competition. I told them that we were holding open "auditions" for five writing spots on our blog. I had anyone who was interested submit Word docs or links to some of their best-written work.

I think we had about 150 submissions, from which we narrowed them down to the top 20. At this point, we had each of the top 20 write a blog post for us that we would publish on the blog. We then used reader response from those 20 articles to judge and pick the top 10.

We then repeated the process with the top 10 and had them publish another article. Judging from reader response, we narrowed it down to our five winners.

This was very much the "American Idol" style contest, and it was wonderful for a bunch of reasons:

- We let the readers tell us who they wanted to see more of rather than have me trying to decide on the five best from the 150.

- The writers likely spread the word to their friends and family about what they were doing, which, in turn, increased our brand awareness, as well as social shares, etc.

- We got weeks' worth of great content from writers who were writing the best possible article they could.

It was fun for the writers and me, and the community seemed to enjoy it, too.

Some people assume you need a huge audience to do something like this, and while you do need an audience, I don't think it necessarily needs to be large at all. I have seen a couple of other much smaller blogs run similar contests, and they seemed very effective.

# GRAPHICS AND DESIGN

# WHERE DO I FIND BEAUTIFUL, FREE IMAGES?

A handful of good options for you to use are free or cheap. First, let's talk about the creative commons license. Simply put, these are free images to use as long as you link within the blog post to the source. You should probably read the full details of the license, but this is the gist of it.

To find free creative commons images, you can just go to: http://search.creativecommons.org

Compfight.com is another great way to find CC images, and they even provide the HTML code allowing you to give credit that you can just copy and paste into your blog post.

You will find there are some good images with the CC license for some niches and very little to choose from for other niches. So, if you want to step up your game and begin buying images, these are some of my favorite cheap options:

Photodune.net – They don't have the biggest supply

yet, but typically the photos are better quality images than some of the other cheap stock photography sites. You can find images for as cheap as $1 a piece.

Dreamstime.com – This site has a huge supply of stock photos, some good, and a lot of mediocre ones mixed in. You can find images as cheap as $0.20 a download.

istockphoto.com – These guys are expensive, but they have great images and lots of them. So if you need a high-quality image, this is the place to go.

# HOW CAN I EDIT MY PHOTOS WITHOUT PHOTOSHOP?

I started using Photoshop years ago, and I still do for most of my photo editing. But there are so many great free options out there. For almost anything you want to do for your blog images you don't need Photoshop. Here are some of my favorite alternatives.

Gimp.org – This is an open-source (and FREE) piece of software that you can download that does 99 percent of what Photoshop can do. It's high-powered, so for simple editing like cropping or adding text, I would probably use a more basic tool.

Picmonkey.com – This is a great website that allows you to make a ton of edits to your photos all for free, although they offer a premium version with additional features. Whenever I'm not using Photoshop, this is my go-to tool.

ipiccy.com – This one is about as close to a Web-based Photoshop alternative as you can get. This is a high-powered tool that can do a lot, all from your browser.

idpinthat.com – If you're looking for images to use in your blog posts and would like to overlay them with text, this is just what you're looking for.

canva.com – This site is great for creating Pinterest-friendly graphics, and they have tons of templates you can use to make the process a lot easier.

# HOW DO I GET A LOGO THAT LOOKS LIKE I PAID $1,000 FOR IT?

Let me start by saying that good logo designers are great at what they do and can really dramatically help you improve the professional image of your site/business. However, for bloggers who are bootstrapping it, there are many ways to still get a great looking logo for not very much money.

## 99Designs.com

I used 99Designs, the crowdsourcing design website, for a logo I needed a few years ago. The way it works is that you say what kind of logo you're looking for, and designers submit logos (over the course of seven days) for your approval. You then get the opportunity to pick your favorite as the winner.

If you don't get a design you love you can get 100 percent of your money refunded. Needless to say, I didn't have anything to lose trying it out, so I did.

The minimum amount you can offer for a design is $295. I decided I wanted to motivate the designers a little bit more, so I offered $30 extra at $325. To my surprise, four days later, we still didn't have a single entry.

The first entry came in on day five and was pretty bad. And we didn't really start getting many other entries until about day six, and still, most of them were pretty bad. To make matters worse, NONE of the designers actually read what I was telling them I wanted in the logo. I was very specific about a few things, and I'm not sure if they just didn't care or didn't read it, but either way none of them hit the mark.

After the seven days were up, we had 38 entries from about 20 designers, yet it was still a very easy decision to ask for our money back. So I called 99Designs and had to leave a voicemail since all the operators were busy and about three or four hours later, I got a call back and got my money refunded.

In theory, I love the idea of 99Designs, but looking back now, I honestly feel a little guilty that all those people worked, and none of them got paid a dime. Granted, they all knew the risk they were taking and some of them did VERY LITTLE work, but the process seems a very inefficient one.

The 99designs logo templates

On another note, 99Designs has another interesting

product/service, logo templates for $100. These beautiful and well-designed logos just plug into your website or company name. After purchasing the design, you tell the designers what you want the logo to say, what color you want it, etc., and they make the simple and quick customizations for you.

Some of them are pretty good looking logos. These are some examples of the logos you can have customized:

COMPANY NAME

While others have used some of them since it's a usage license, for the yet-to-be purchased logos, the site allows you to purchase an exclusive license for $300. So, my thinking is that service won't work for every business, but for most small business owners and bloggers, using an option like this, is a great way to get a very nice-looking logo for $100.

## Graphic River logo templates

GraphicRiver.net has a bunch of logo templates that you can have tweaked (text and colors changed) for even less than 99Designs. At the time of this writing, the site doesn't have as large a selection as 99Designs, but it does have a bunch of gorgeous ones for sale for about $30.

# WHAT SHOULD I HAVE IN MY BLOG'S SIDEBAR?

The specifics of the answer differ, depending on your niche, but the general rule most likely is the same.

You need to ask yourself two questions when evaluating what to include in your sidebar:

- What are your most important current goals?
- What will help your readers?

## Your current goals

Are you trying to:

- Build your email list?
- Make more money with ads?
- Grow your Facebook page?
- Communicate what your site is all about?
- Increase the stickiness of your blog?
- Point visitors to a particular page on your site?
- Increase your Pinterest following?
- Show social proof to visitors to "validate" your

blog in their eyes?
- Sell a product you offer?

If you're like most bloggers, you probably want to do most of these things. Now, you need to figure out what's most important to you. Think long-term; don't just exclusively focus on making more money now by plastering 10 ads in your sidebar. Sure, you may squeeze a few more bucks this month by doing so, but it will hurt all your other goals. And most of those other goals, while they may not directly contribute to earnings this month, will play a big part in the long-term earning potential of your site.

I suggest listing these items (and whatever other goals you have) in your sidebar in order of importance to you. And it can change regularly with little consequence because it's pretty quick and simple to move items around in the sidebar.

So, if I'm making a focused push to enlarge my email list this month, I will move that up to the highest position on the page. Maybe next month I want to focus on my Pinterest following, so that will move up the list.

Generally speaking, the higher up an item is in the sidebar, the more people will see it. So, it's pretty simple, just focus on moving your highest priority goals higher up on the sidebar.

## What will help your readers?

Now that you have your goals figured out, you need

to spend some time thinking about what will help your readers. How can you use your sidebar to better help them reach their goals?

Maybe by having:

- Basic navigation (if it isn't in your header) to help them find their way around your site better
- Your most popular articles displayed
- A search box to help readers find older articles
- Space between each widget so it isn't stressful for a reader to see everything crammed together in your sidebar

If there are elements here that would help your readers reach their goals, you need to strongly consider working them in. After all, is the blog for you or your readers?

When focusing on my sidebar (or any part of my site layout for that matter), I always try to balance my goals and my readers' goals and lean toward what will benefit my readers. Gaining a reader who will become a true fan is a worthwhile and valuable goal. It may take a while before it results in money in your pocket, but that doesn't make it any less important.

## A tool to help the process

Crazyegg.com is really good for finding out what readers are actually clicking on.

All you need to do is put a little line of script on your

website to start the test, and after a little while, you can view a heat map overlay of your site, seeing exactly where (and with what frequency) users are clicking your site.

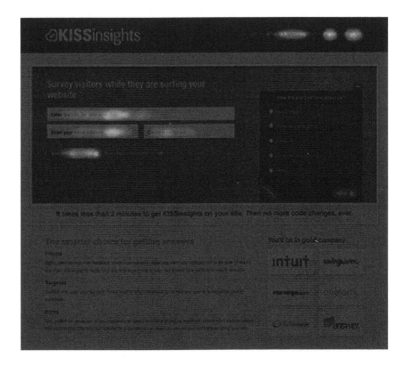

I have gotten some insights from this that I never would have known about. Things like links in my navigation that were never getting clicked. With the insight that CrazyEgg provided I was able to remove them. At the same time, I found some items that needed to be featured a bit more (based on reader click response) because they were kind of hidden.

# HOW TO CREATE A SIMPLE EBOOK COVER FOR FREE

I often get asked about how I create 3D ebook graphics like this for my ebooks:

The easy way, of course, is to hire someone to do it.

But if you're a DIY person like me and have some aptitude for making things look decent, here's my simple process.

1. I start by going to a stock photography site like photodune.net or dreamstime.com and find the best-looking image I can find that fits the topic of my book. In the above example, the obvious image choice would be a stack of money or something, but as much as people are drawn to images of money, there's something magnetic about smiling people. I liked this image, and they're happy because they saved a bunch of money reading my ebook. ;)

2. Then I just pop open Photoshop or Picmonkey.com (if I'm not at my desktop) and find a nice font and write my title in a way that looks good over the image. I often play around with this with multiple tries until I find something that works best.

3. At this point, I now have a 2D (or flat) ebook cover, which is fine, but you can really make it pop a little more and draw more attention by making it look 3D. The simplest way I have found to do this is to use a tool like myecovermaker.com.

Using it has saved me a lot of time and has helped me come up with some graphics that look a whole lot better than I could have done on my own.

The tool allows you to upload an image file and then it automatically converts it into a downloadable ebook cover for you – all in about five minutes.

# The free ebook covers

The site has five different covers you can choose from that are completely free.

Also, there are about 40 other options you can get that are only $4.95. These are just a few of the other cheap ebook cover options.

# So how does it all work?

Start by going to the website MyEcoverMaker.com. Once you get there, you can just click the link that says "Create Ecover." Once you do that, the ball will start rolling.

From this point, you can choose the format you like (ebook, software, video, CD covers, etc.). Next, the site will ask you to upload the image you created in step 2, or you can design it completely from the site. Once the image uploads, you can crop it and see how it will look as an ecover.

Once you complete your crop, you can upload additional pictures or add text. The text editor actually gives you many options to use with a variety of fonts, and it has a bunch of text effects, as well. I particularly like how you can drag, drop, and resize images and text on the cover. These steps make the process pretty simple.

Once you're satisfied with the layout, just hit the "Finalize" button, and it will generate your free (or cheap, depending on which you choose) ebook cover. It then also gives you the option to put it on a transparent background, as well.

# EMAIL MARKETING

# WHAT EMAIL SERVICE PROVIDER DO YOU RECOMMEND?

For a long time I recommended Mailchimp for new bloggers because the site allows new bloggers to start for free. But after a recent experience with them, I now recommend GetResponse.

If you're currently using Mailchimp or want to read my frustrating story, just continue reading. If you want a great email service provider that provides great customer service, just go to GetResponse and move on to the next chapter.

A couple of months ago, Mailchimp caused me a lot of pain and frustration.

Unfortunately, I had been telling everyone about them because they were the only email newsletter service I knew of that was free for the first 2,000 subscribers.

It's a beautifully designed site, and it's easy to use. So

what's not to love?

Well, I used the service for about three years and had some customer service issues in the past but none bad enough to make me want to leave.

Then, it happened.

*(A little back story: My email lists are a big part of my business. I have several auto-responders I use to send my email courses that we have thousands of students taking at any given moment.)*

I was on my first day of vacation actually, and I had said I wasn't going to check email, but for some reason, I happened to peek into Gmail to find an email from Mailchimp saying they had shut down my account, and because I had been sending spam email they wouldn't reinstate my account.

So, I decided to call customer support and see what the deal was. Then, I realized Mailchimp does NOT have ANY phone support – only email support.

At that moment, I knew this wasn't good. Email Service Providers (ESPs) have so much spam to deal with that they don't have time to give you much consideration once they blacklist you.

I immediately sent a support ticket, of course, telling the support personnel how urgent it was.

Then, I waited. One day. Two days.

At this point, after a lot of digging, I discovered that they had a chat box!

I thought this would be great since I could now talk to a real person, but they quickly informed me that they can not provide any assistance in cases like mine.

I sent in another support ticket.

At this point, my email courses were a mess because people weren't receiving their lessons each day, and the students began emailing me asking what was going on.

Then another day went by.

By now, I was frantically searching for another email service provider and saw GetResponse has excellent customer support.

Finally, the next day (four days later), I got an email from Mailchimp that said, oops our fault, your account was incorrectly flagged for spam, but you didn't do anything wrong, so your account is reinstated.

By now, I was so furious I knew it was time to go.

Moral of the story: If you use Mailchimp, be very careful. Not having phone support and having a four-day turnaround time on email support for URGENT, business-hindering matters is something to keep in mind.

# So where did I end up going?

After researching about five to six different ESPs, I decided on GetResponse mostly because it has outstanding chat, phone, and email support. I have now talked to support people about 10 times. I just love these guys.

The other big factor for me was the user interface and ease of use. GetResponse hit it out the park here, as well. Mailchimp was very good in this department, but GetResponse is just as good.

If you're a Mailchimp user, I hope you never have an issue that needs support, but if you ever decide to make a switch, check out GetResponse.

# WHY YOU MUST BEGIN BUILDING YOUR EMAIL LIST NOW

I don't really have any regrets about how I built my blog, but if there was one thing I would do differently if I were starting now, it's to immediately start building an email list.

This may sound obvious, but it took me about three years to realize that most people who come to our blogs are NOT coming back. Even most of the ones who find your blog genuinely interesting will not return.

But rather than get discouraged by that fact, we need to embrace it and do our best to "lock in" with as many of our readers as possible. In my estimation, getting them on our email lists is the best way to stay connected with a reader.

In my case, about three years into my blogging journey, it dawned on me that my only goal with the millions of visitors we had up to that point was to get a click on an ad to make a few bucks. But what about after the click? Was I ever going to earn from all those visitors again? Of course not. Clearly, this was very short-sighted thinking.

As it started to sink in, I imagined how many of those visitors I could have turned into email subscribers if I had just tried. But I didn't even try, and so, they came, they left, and I likely never heard from them again.

In the volatile Google environment that bloggers now live in, you could lose 75 percent of your traffic overnight (I have friends who have lived through this), so having large, dependable traffic source, your email list, is a great idea.

Don't make the mistake I made. Get focused on building your email list today.

At the time of this writing, we have about 54,000 email subscribers, and we're currently getting about a 1.4 percent conversion rate of site visitors to the email list. While I'm very excited to have an email list as large as it is, I know that we've had more than 22 million visitors since we began the site.

If we would have tried to grow our email list from the beginning and got even a 1 percent conversion rate all along we'd have an email list of roughly 220,000 rather than the 54,000 we actually have.

As I said earlier, I don't have regrets; I learned a ton all along this journey, and some of the lessons I had to learn the hard way. But, do yourself a favor and learn this lesson the easy way and get started today.

# So, how do you get people to subscribe to your email newsletter?

I mentioned our 1.4 percent conversion rate of our visitors to our email lists in the previous chapter, and, depending on your niche, you can probably do a lot better than that.

Regardless, it took us a while to get it up to that point. Below are some of the most important things we did to help us increase it to 1.4 percent.

This may seem obvious, but the way to getting more people to subscribe comes down to just a couple of things:

1. Give them a compelling reason to subscribe – offering something free like an ebook, printable cheat sheet/checklist, video of exclusive content, etc. From my testing, offering something always drastically increases signups.

2. Ask and ask often. If you really want to increase your email list, I would suggest having a subscribe box at the end of every post and make it big. Of course, have one in the sidebar. And if you really want to get a lot of subscribers, consider doing a delayed popup form.

I have mixed feelings about the popups, but some of the plugins now give you more ability to customize the settings, which allows you to make them considerably less annoying. For example, some plugins allow you to put a time delay so that the popups only appear to people who are really enjoying the article. Some only pop up at the end of the post, which is a great time for it to pop up. Some even allow you to select which posts, pages, and categories the popup appears in.

The important takeaway is that popups work. On my site, my conversion rate nearly doubled overnight when I added a delayed popup.

Here are a couple of premium plugins to consider that allow you to add signup forms on your site as well as popup options:

- Hybrid Connect
- Optin Monster

# ADDITIONAL QUESTIONS

# HOW DO I KEEP INAPPROPRIATE ADS OFF MY SITE?

Keeping unwanted ads off your site can be challenging, depending on which ad networks you use, but by using Adsense ads, I have greatly reduced the number of inappropriate ads that show up.

1. Adsense gives you a tremendous amount of control over what types of ads that show up as well as letting you blacklist any that sneak through.

Just by logging in your account and clicking the "Allow & Block Ads" link at the top, you can toggle simple checkboxes that allow you to select which categories of ads you would like to block from showing.

2. For many years, I had a little link below each ad unit that read, "Click to report inappropriate ad." I didn't want to wholly trust in Adsense and its filters, so I figured I would enlist the help of my readers to help me catch any inappropriate ads.

It turns out the Adsense filter is pretty good. In the

seven years I've been blogging, I received a total of three or four emails from readers bringing shady ads to my attention. Because I asked them for the ad URL, I could quickly go into my Adsense dashboard, blacklist that site, and prevent it from ever showing again.

# WHY A BLOG IS A TERRIBLE TOOL TO DELIVER INFORMATION AND WHY YOU NEED TO WORK TO FIX THIS

Over the years, it has become more apparent to me that a blog is just a terrible way to teach people. What normally happens is that a blogger starts a blog covering the basics with blog posts that are great for the beginner, and then, as the following grows and as the blogger gains even more expertise, they begin writing more and more complex articles that may no longer be suitable for a beginner. Bloggers often become susceptible to the "curse of knowledge" when they forget what they didn't know when they began, and they tend to assume that everyone has a certain level of knowledge.

This is all fine and dandy if you start with 100 beginners and only take those 100 on a five-year journey with you as you progress. But the reality is that most people who will ever come to your blog are beginners, and after three, five, or seven years (in my case), you will likely have a blog that isn't very suitable for beginners. If you prove me wrong, I applaud you, but I have seen this happen way too many times to count.

## So what's the solution?

There are actually many ways to help remedy this problem, but for the sake of brevity, I will focus on what I've done and what has worked for me.

## 1. The easiest solution: a Start Here page.

I honestly think EVERY blog should have this after they have 20 blog posts up. The purpose of the page is for someone who lands on your site, who maybe knows nothing about your topic, but wants to learn.

Imagine someone emailing you and saying, "Hey, I'm interested in learning more about (your topic), and I have no idea where to begin. What do you recommend?"

Let this page be a guide that points them to the articles or resources on your site that a beginner needs. Also, don't be afraid to link to other books, online courses, articles elsewhere around the Web if they will help. If you don't know how to adequately answer that imaginary email from a reader, then congratulations, you now have some much needed work to do and probably a ton of blog post ideas to get going on.

## 2. An ebook

If you have a single blog post that covers the basics for a beginner or maybe a series of blog posts, you could easily turn this into a downloadable PDF ebook for your audience.

All you really need to do is copy and paste the content into Google Docs, format it so it looks nice, and then click File > Download As > PDF Document.

Then, just go upload this as a media file in the WordPress Admin, and next you can point people to that link to download it.

Obviously, you can take this up a notch by getting it designed by someone on Elance.com, but for phase 1, this is a great and easy way to get it out the door.

## 3. An email course

I did this a couple of years ago and am really happy I did. I started by creating a 20-day free email course for my readers that takes them through a lot of the basics of money management.

I strongly considered charging for it (and have had many people surprised that it's free), but I knew I could get a lot more people to take the course if it was free. My mission with the site is to help as many people as possible and pay the bills at the same time.

These are the big advantages I love about the course.

It actually helps people.

The feedback I get is incredibly encouraging. I occasionally get emails from people saying how a blog post changed their lives, but I regularly get it about the course, which ironically is just a bunch of blog posts packaged together. This is good for me as a blogger because there's no better way to keep readers thinking about your blog than to have a measurable impact on their lives.

It builds the email list.

Since growing my email list is one of my top priorities, this just works perfectly. Everyone who signs up for our free course gets automatically added to our email list.

It adds revenue.

I chose to keep the lessons on the site rather than to put them in the emails themselves. This way when someone clicks the link in the email to get the lesson, she'll come back to the site, see the ads, and I make money that way.

Anyway, bottom line, I love it. To me, it's a huge win for the readers as they get a digestible package of content that they need for FREE while I build my email list and still make money from the ads.

# SHOULD I PUT MY EMAIL ADDRESS ON MY CONTACT PAGE?

I would suggest it, but if you don't, at least make sure you have a working contact form.

I use a combination of my email address and a contact form (using the Contact Form 7 plugin). The big argument for having your email address listed is that many people won't use a contact form, which may be a good thing, depending on what your goals are.

I have heard that many media contacts don't like using a contact form and pretty much only contact those with email addresses and phone numbers. So, if you're looking for big media exposure, that's something to keep in mind.

Also, having an address and phone number listed on your contact page adds credibility and legitimacy to your business in Google's eyes, too.

# WHAT ARE THE BEST WAYS TO CONNECT WITH OTHERS IN MY NICHE?

Connecting with others in your niche is one of the most important things for bloggers to do for so many reasons. No one is an island, and you need help to get where you want to go. I'm very confident my blog would be nowhere near what it is today without connecting to many other bloggers in my niche. From collaboration ideas, to guest posting, to helping promote each other, to encouragement, etc., it has been incredibly valuable having a community of folks to reach out to. Not to mention, some of my best friendships today are a result of these connections.

## So how do I do it?

How you do it depends and is different for every niche, but you need to find where the others are hanging out and congregating. In my niche, there are private forums where many of the bloggers hang out, there are Facebook groups, an industry conference (FinCon), and of course, at the blogs themselves.

If I were just starting in a new niche and wanted to connect with and get to know some of the bloggers doing what I'm doing, I would:

1. Google "Your niche" + forums and check out those communities.

2. Do a search for Facebook groups with bloggers in your niche.

Start by going to Facebook and then searching for your topic in the Facebook search bar. Next, click "see more results" as shown below:

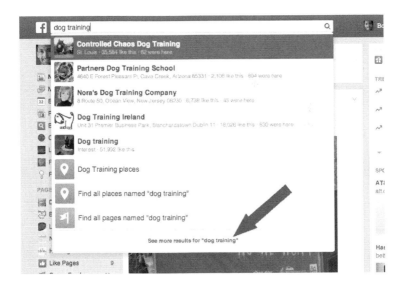

Next, click the groups tab as shown below:

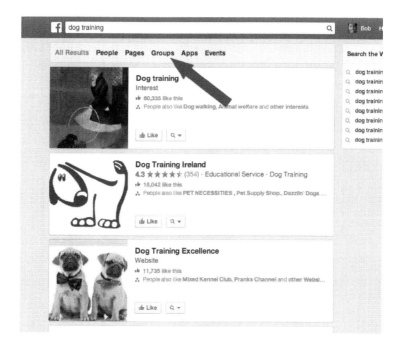

Now you will find all kinds of related groups for you to join!

3. Email some of your favorite bloggers and ask them whether there are any conferences or meet-ups they attend.

4. And, of course, commenting on the blogs is a great way to get on their radar, as well.

# I FEEL LIKE QUITTING MY BLOG. WHAT SHOULD I DO?

Sometimes we need help to stay encouraged when times are tough. During the past seven years, I have saved every remotely encouraging email I receive from readers. I knew there would be days when I'd feel like quitting or when I felt as if no one was reading or no one was being helped. On those days, it's really nice to pop open that folder and just read email after email of readers who my blog genuinely had an impact on.

Obviously, this is just one simple idea that may help, but without getting too philosophical, you really have to remember why you started blogging in the first place. If it was for money, I'm sorry because you have a tough road ahead of you. It's not that earning money shouldn't be a goal, but if it's the only goal, then you're in trouble.

I can speak for myself and almost every other professional blogger I know and say that we began blogging because we had a passion about a topic that we just really wanted to share. We really wanted to help readers, provide insight instead of confusion, and really make the world a little bit better. For most of us, the money was icing on an already great cake.

My point is I'm confident that if I were only blogging for the money, I'd have returned to my old day job by now. It's just too easy to quit. You have to have a better reason to write.

Assuming you do have a better reason to write, think back on why you started it and think back on the good memories. Try not to dwell on the negatives and definitely stop comparing your blog to all the rock-star bloggers. That doesn't do any good at all.

And don't be afraid to take a break! It's much better for you to take a couple of weeks off from writing to rejuvenate, than to spend months writing half-hearted posts.

Remember, feeling discouraged is just part of the creative process. Just keep on keeping on!

# WHAT ARE MY CHANCES OF BECOMING A PROFESSIONAL BLOGGER?

I get emails with this question a lot. It isn't necessarily a bad question, but it's a nearly impossible question to answer, and I think there are some things to consider, also.

First, I've done this long enough and have coached enough bloggers over the years that I can say with a very high certainty that very few will ever end up as professional bloggers. But, for me to say, or even guess, who will succeed (assuming that's the goal) and who won't is not fair.

Just like anyone else, I've failed at more things than I care to count, and I've had a handful of "successes." There were some bloggers who I thought had terrible ideas, and they ended up doing very well. On the other hand, there are cases when I was sure someone had what it took to grow a massive following, and it appears I was very wrong.

We have to put this whole thing in proper perspective. It's entrepreneurship and starting a business. Sure, many businesses fail and a lot of them just don't have great ideas, but I'm convinced that so much of what we call success is more a matter of execution than the great idea.

You have to remember one good idea carried to completion is better than 1,000 great ideas given up on.

*"Our greatest weakness lies in giving up. The most certain way to succeed is always to try just one more time."* – Thomas A. Edison

Getting back to the question... Just because the odds aren't great in terms of how likely the rest of the world is to succeed doesn't mean you won't. And even if you don't make it full-time, making a part-time income doing something you love isn't too bad, either.

# WHAT ARE THE COMMON TRAITS OF SUCCESSFUL BLOGGERS?

People always answer questions like the chapter title with very vague and generic answers like "authenticity," "only write what you're passionate about," etc. And while I 100 percent agree with these ideas, I just want to be the oddball who actually points out some slightly more specific things I've noticed tend to play a big part in many bloggers' successes.

The truth is that each blogger does better with some of these than others, and this section isn't for us to dwell on how poorly we're doing in some of these areas. The goal is just to point out the elements that seem to be common denominators with many successful bloggers.

They're absolutely not requirements for success, just common trends. So, I'm really trying to inspire you to try to improve in some areas, but don't get discouraged by the list. Deal?

# The obvious: great content

It should go without saying, but it's worthy of repeating: You have to create great stuff. Without it, you leave readers disappointed, and they have no incentive to come back.

Defining "great" isn't really that easy. It all depends. It may be short content; it may be long content. Most of the time, I would say that long and thorough is better than short, but there are certain niches where a long and thorough explanation is looked down upon, and a quick and dirty explanation is favorable, maybe a website geared toward teens?

Lots of pictures are often a good thing, but there are instances when a video is much more valuable. Instructional videos are often much more helpful to the reader than even the most detailed instructional photos.

Rather than getting caught up trying to deconstruct what makes good content, let's step back and take a simpler approach.

Great content is something someone bookmarks and/or shares.

Think about the type of content you share on social media sites. What are the articles, photos, videos, that you just can't help but share with others?

This is the content you want to create. When you

finish the article, ask yourself (as objectively as possible), "If I were a reader of my blog, would I feel absolutely compelled to share this or bookmark it for future reference?" If you answer is a resounding yes, then you've created great content.

## Great titles/headlines

As much as I hate to say it, if you can write captivating and magnetic titles, you can get people to your site, even if your content isn't great. That's why when you can work these two elements together, you can get visitors to your blog and then convert them to regulars.

Great headlines are different, depending on your audience, but for some great template ideas that will work in many niches, Brian Clark has a great list here:

http://www.copyblogger.com/10-sure-fire-headline-formulas-that-work

## Beautiful images

Pinterest leads the charge to make the Internet more visually appealing, and most successful bloggers I see use beautiful images. Even if you don't have good ones, just making sure that each post has at least some kind of image helps.

Facebook has concluded that people share posts with images a lot more than just text posts. And obviously getting Pinterest traffic is next to impossible without an image and is very difficult with a mediocre image. Spending focused time on each blog post looking for great looking and eye-catching images is becoming more important.

## Humor

Have you ever noticed when you're with a stranger and one of you makes a joke, it creates an instant bond of trust?

For some reason, laughter and jokes really can help us feel comfortable with others. I have seen many bloggers use this to their advantage to connect with an otherwise unconnected reader.

As if that weren't enough, we live in a troubled world right now and people seem to be reaching for any opportunity to get a quick laugh to lighten the mood.

## Marketing focus

Most successful bloggers I know focus at least 50 percent of their time on marketing and getting the word out about their blogs and blog posts. They create great content but spend less than half their time doing it. They spend the majority of their time getting eyeballs to the content.

On the opposite end of the spectrum, I see many new bloggers just start writing, and then they write some more, and then even more. Waiting, waiting, and waiting for the traffic to start rolling in. And it doesn't. Some times their content is even great stuff, but they just don't spend the energy to get visitors to see the content.

For bloggers stuck in this rut, I suggest taking half the content that you're already writing and use it as guest posts for other sites. This is a simple way to jump-start your marketing efforts. Use 50 percent of your content on your site and 50 percent on other relevant sites/blogs linking with a bio-line linking to your site.

# WHY YOUR BLOG MATTERS

I'm fully convinced that each of us has something to share. There's something in each of us the world needs to hear.

Without getting too "Tony Robbins" on you, you have a unique set of gifts, skills, and experiences that allow you to offer some insight on something that few others can.

I can't even begin to tell you how many authors, bloggers, songwriters, poets, and other writers who have had an impact on my life. You can never underestimate the power of what you're writing.

Even if you're only reaching 100 people each month, if you're having a life-changing impact on their lives, isn't it worth it?

So do yourself this favor: Whether you have a huge blog or only get a handful of visitors at this point, don't get caught up in the numbers.

Your effectiveness is not equal to the number of page views your blog gets.

Keep writing and working hard to deeply affect the lives of your readers and keep changing the world one blog post at a time.

# THANK YOU FOR READING

I want to thank you again for picking up this book and I appreciate you more than you know!

If you found this book helpful at all, I'd be incredibly grateful if you could leave a review at Amazon.

You may not be aware that independent authors are battling against all the books with million-dollar advertising budgets at Amazon, and reviews are a huge help for indie authors like me!

Either way, I still appreciate your picking up the book, and I hope it helps move you forward on your blogging journey!

You can find links to all the resources mentioned in this book at BlogBusiness101.com/links.

Feel free to email additional questions to me at bob@BlogBusiness101.com.

If you'd like to receive more tips like these listed in this book, you can join our email list at BlogBusiness101.com.

I wish you all the best!
Bob

# NOTES

Made in the USA
Middletown, DE
23 November 2014